U.S. Overseas Military Presence

What Are the Strategic Choices?

Lynn E. Davis, Stacie L. Pettyjohn,
Melanie W. Sisson, Stephen M. Worman,
Michael J. McNerney

Prepared for the United States Air Force
Approved for public release; distribution unlimited

PROJECT AIR FORCE

The research described in this report was sponsored by the United States Air Force under Contract FA7014-06-C-0001. Further information may be obtained from the Strategic Planning Division, Directorate of Plans, Hq USAF.

Library of Congress Cataloging-in-Publication Data

U.S. overseas military presence : what are the strategic choices? / Lynn E. Davis ... [et al.].
       p. cm.
    Includes bibliographical references.
    ISBN 978-0-8330-7340-2 (pbk. : alk. paper)
    1. United States—Armed Forces—Foreign countries. 2. Military bases, American—Foreign countries. 3. United States—Defenses—Planning. 4. National security—United States—Planning. 5. United States—Military policy—Planning. 6. Strategy. I. Davis, Lynn E. (Lynn Etheridge), 1943-

    UA26.A2U75 2012
    355'.033573—dc23

                                                                          2012031923

Published 2012 by the RAND Corporation
1776 Main Street, P.O. Box 2138, Santa Monica, CA 90407-2138
1200 South Hayes Street, Arlington, VA 22202-5050
4570 Fifth Avenue, Suite 600, Pittsburgh, PA 15213-2665
RAND URL: http://www.rand.org/
To order RAND documents or to obtain additional information, contact
Distribution Services: Telephone: (310) 451-7002;
Fax: (310) 451-6915; Email: order@rand.org

Preface

The United States will need to design its overseas military presence for the coming decades in a way that responds to the changing international security environment and that takes into account a view on how the United States should see its future role in the world. Focusing on different perspectives on the role that overseas U.S. military presence can play in achieving global U.S. security interests, we developed alternative global postures and illustrated them with the associated U.S. Air Force bases, combat and mobility forces, active-duty personnel, and operating costs. We then used these to define critical strategic choices that policymakers will confront in defining overseas U.S. military presence.

The research reported here is the product of a fiscal year 2011 RAND Project AIR FORCE research study, "Air Power, Command of the Commons, and Global Posture." This research was sponsored by the Deputy Director of Strategic Planning, Headquarters U.S. Air Force (HQ USAF/A8X) and was conducted in the Strategy and Doctrine Program of RAND Project AIR FORCE.

This monograph will be of interest to policymakers across the U.S. government responsible for designing U.S. overseas military presence and to those engaged in debates over the future role of the United States overseas.

RAND Project Air Force

RAND Project AIR FORCE (PAF), a division of the RAND Corporation, is the U.S. Air Force's federally funded research and development center for studies and analyses. PAF provides the Air Force with independent analyses of policy alternatives affecting the development, employment, combat readiness, and support of current and future air, space, and cyber forces. Research is conducted in four programs: Force Modernization and Employment; Manpower, Personnel, and Training; Resource Management; and Strategy and Doctrine.

Additional information about PAF is available on our website: http://www.rand.org/paf/

Contents

Figures

Tables

Summary

Since World War II, the United States has relied on a network of global military bases and forces to provide forward, collective defense against the Soviet Union, to counter the proliferation of weapons of mass destruction, and to fight terrorism. Today, the international environment has changed, with China asserting itself across East Asia, Iran pursuing an ambitious nuclear program, and al-Qaeda affiliates still presenting threats to Western interests. Domestically, too, the environment is changing as the United States confronts serious economic uncertainties and growing pressures have resulted in reductions in government spending, including spending on defense.

Indeed, a debate is under way as to the future role of America in the world. One aspect of this debate is what the size and characteristics of future U.S. overseas military presence should be, with the Obama administration calling for a global presence that emphasizes the Asia-Pacific and the Middle East, while maintaining defense commitments to Europe.[1] Other voices are calling for bringing most U.S. military forces home.[2] This monograph seeks to inform the overall debate and support future policymakers by introducing a new analytical approach to defining future overseas U.S. military presence.

Our approach begins with U.S. global security interests and then focuses on the specific threats to them in East Asia, Europe, and the

---

[1] U.S. Department of Defense, Sustaining U.S. Global Leadership: Priorities for 21st Century Defense, January 2012, pp. 1–3.

[2] Senator Carl Levin reportedly said that he will not support closing bases in the United States until bases are closed in Europe (Elisabeth Bumiller and Thom Shanker, "Defense Budget Cuts Would Limit Raises and Close Bases," *New York Times*, January 26, 2012).

Middle East. It recognizes that policymakers and those in the public debate hold different perspectives on what overseas U.S. military presence is needed. So, we designed global postures that differ in their perspectives, or strategic view, and illustrated them in terms of the necessary U.S. Air Force bases, combat and mobility forces, active-duty personnel, and base operating costs. What emerged from our analyses are the critical strategic choices that policymakers need to address and that the public needs to debate as they consider future overseas U.S. military presence.

The first strategic choice is for the United States to decide whether its overseas military presence can be reduced and diversified because its allies in Europe and Northeast Asia are able, economically and militarily, to assume primary responsibility for their own security. Such a choice could involve, for example, the United States reducing bases and combat forces in the United Kingdom, Germany, Japan, and South Korea. The remaining permanent U.S. overseas presence would provide the bases and military forces for immediate responses to future threats and thereby reassure U.S. allies and partners. The United States would then have the flexibility to expand its rotational presence across Southeast and Southwest Asia if threats were to increase or if partners were to call for reassurance.

If relying more on U.S. allies seems risky, given their reliance on nonmilitary strategies for responding to potential military threats and the political and economic constraints on their defense spending, the United States would face other strategic choices with respect to its future overseas military presence. One is whether it is time for the United States to rely primarily on U.S.-based forces to respond to global crises and conflicts, keeping only a small global forward presence to reassure allies and partners. Such a choice would be based on the perspective that deterring and responding to China, North Korea, and Iran in the future will depend not on overseas presence but rather on the capabilities of U.S. military forces at home to be able to surge into the regions in the event of crises or conflict. This would be the case for reassuring U.S. allies and partners as well. Such a choice would involve the United States relying on mobility forces and bases overseas, plus only a few combat forces, and seeking access to bases more globally were threats from China and Iran to expand. Transitioning U.S. military forces to the United States would have the advantage of reducing their vulnerability to expanding missile threats.

Choosing to reduce overseas U.S. military presence does not make sense if the perspective is that overseas U.S. presence plays an important role in deterring and responding to one or more of the threats that China, North Korea, and Iran pose and in reassuring U.S. allies and partners. The strategic choice that then arises is whether the United States should maintain its global posture essentially as today and prepare to increase its overseas presence in Southeast and Southwest Asia if threats expand. Keeping existing bases would have the advantage of reducing the risks associated with not being able to return to bases once given up.

Such a robust global posture could become too expensive or politically problematic in some countries. So, the final strategic choice is whether the United States should focus its overseas U.S. presence more on Asia (because of the need to influence China's expanding military activities) or on the Middle East (because of the threats to stability and the flow of oil from a potentially nuclear-armed Iran). Choosing to emphasize Asia would involve keeping planned bases and military forces in Japan and South Korea, then expanding rotational deployments and exercises to the extent they become politically feasible with countries in Southeast Asia. Choosing to emphasize the Middle East would have the United States rely more on surging military forces from the United States for contingencies in Asia and keeping bases in the Gulf Cooperation Council states and Africa to be able to blunt quickly any attacks on U.S. partners and to provide reassurance. In each of these cases, the choice would involve reorienting the focus of U.S. military forces in Europe to be able to surge forces from the United States to respond to crises and conflicts in the region where U.S. presence was reduced.

There is no one right strategic choice, but in our view, those involved in debates on the future global U.S. posture need to make explicit their implicit underlying perspectives on what role overseas military presence can play in achieving U.S. global security interests and then make decisions based on this menu of strategic choices. This makes it possible that future U.S. overseas military presence can be based on agreement on how well it serves U.S. global security interests and not on other, unrelated considerations, as is often the case today.

Acknowledgments

We would like to thank Michael Maxwell, our sponsor in the Air Force, who has given us counsel and support throughout our research and analyses, along with others on the Air Staff, who have reviewed our briefings and provided insights into Air Force planning. We appreciate the support of many RAND colleagues, especially Andrew Hoehn, who worked with us closely throughout our project and offered extremely helpful comments and critiques. We gained, too, from seminars and discussions with those involved in parallel projects on the Air Force posture in different regions of the world: Alan Vick, David Frelinger, David Orletsky, Andrew Scobell, Jennifer Moroney, and David Thaler. Thanks to Perry Firoz and Michael Boito, who were very helpful in our putting together the database of overseas Air Force personnel and current Air Force base operating costs. Our appreciation goes to PAF Strategy and Doctrine Program Director, Paula Thornhill, who worked with us closely in the design of our analysis framework and in our briefings to the senior Air Force leadership. We also benefited greatly from the careful and thoughtful comments provided by our reviewers, David Thaler and Barry Pavel. Linda Walgamott was essential to our success, in helping with the myriad of administrative details necessary to the conduct of our project, and we thank her especially. Thank you goes to Phyllis Gilmore, our editor, who did a terrific job with our manuscript. This monograph is improved by all their contributions.

Abbreviations

AB	air base
AMC	Air Mobility Command
CSL	cooperative security location
DoD	Department of Defense
FOS	forward operating site
GCC	Gulf Cooperation Council
JTAGS	joint tactical ground station
JTF	joint task force
MOB	main operating base
NAF	naval air facility
NATO	North Atlantic Treaty Organization
PAF	Project AIR FORCE
RAF	Royal Air Force
ROK	Republic of Korea
SOF	special operations forces
UAE	United Arab Emirates
USAF	U.S. Air Force

CHAPTER ONE

Introduction

Study Objectives and Scope

The current U.S. overseas military is largely the outcome of responses to threats as they emerged historically and over time, in Western Europe and in East Asia to the Soviet Union; in the Middle East to the ambitions, nuclear and otherwise, of Iraq and Iran; and around the world to the hostile activities of al-Qaeda and other terrorist organizations.[1] Today, however, the Soviet Union has transitioned from a peer competitor to something less, while China's economic standing and military capabilities allow it increasingly to challenge U.S. global leadership. The United States has removed the threat of a weapons of mass destruction–armed Iraq, but Iran's nuclear program continues to evolve. The U.S. military relationship with its partners in the Middle East continues to grow, while prospects for change are high as a result of the Arab spring. Although al-Qaeda's putative operational leader and confirmed figurehead, Osama bin Laden, is dead, the ability of terrorist groups to acquire and potentially use disruptive technologies against the United States has grown.

Recognizing these realities and the fact of new resource constraints, President Barack Obama, in his introduction to the Department of Defense's (DoD's) 2012 strategic guidance, stated that the "Nation is at a moment of transition." In the accompanying guidance, the Secretary of Defense commits to continuing a global presence

---

[1] Andrew Krepinevich and Robert O. Work, *A New Global Defense Posture for the Second Transoceanic Era*, Washington, D.C.: Center for Strategic and Budgetary Assessments, 2007.

emphasizing the Asia-Pacific and the Middle East, while maintaining defense commitments to Europe.[2]

The guidance goes on to establish "core national interests" that involve defeating al-Qaeda and its affiliates, deterring and defeating aggression by adversaries, countering weapons of mass destruction, effectively operating in and across all domains, maintaining a safe and effective nuclear deterrent, and protecting the homeland.[3] But it does not link the role of overseas presence directly to achieving these interests. The guidance focuses on military missions for sizing and shaping future U.S. military forces and includes as one of the "shaping" missions for U.S. military forces providing "a stabilizing presence" involving a "sustainable pace of presence operations abroad." In the discussion of this mission, however, the guidance focuses on rotational deployments and bilateral and multilateral training exercises, not a permanent overseas U.S. military presence.[4]

As a result of reductions in the defense budget, the U.S. presence in Europe will be reduced by two Army combat brigades and some smaller units and two USAF squadrons (one combat and one air control).[5] The United States and Australia have agreed to a rotational Marine Corps presence and aircraft deployments in the coming years. The United States is expanding its operational cooperation with Thailand, the Philippines, and Singapore and will be seeking to enhance its partnerships with Indonesia, Malaysia, India, Vietnam, and New Zealand.[6]

The process of defining what U.S. overseas presence is needed is left largely to the regional theater commanders in Europe, Africa, the Middle East, Asia, and Central and South America. The sum of this overseas presence becomes the global U.S. posture.

---

[2]   U.S. Department of Defense (DoD), "Sustaining U.S. Global Leadership: Priorities for 21st Century Defense," Washington, D.C., January 2012.

[3]   DoD, 2012.

[4]   DoD, 2012, pp. 5–6.

[5]   Karen Parrish, "Panetta Outlines U.S. Troop Changes in Europe," press release, U.S. Department of Defense, February 16, 2012.

[6]   Leon E. Panetta, speech delivered at the Shangri-La Hotel, Singapore, June 2, 2012.

There are problems though with such an approach. First, it is difficult to account for threats that are not regional but transnational. Another problem is that the contribution of military forces in one theater is often not considered for operations in other theaters. Finally, a narrow theater focus makes it hard to define an overall strategic view for the global U.S. posture or establish priorities among the theaters.

Another approach to defining the U.S. overseas presence focuses on transnational threats, for example threats to what are called the "global commons": the air, sea, and space domains available for the use of all international actors but owned by none. In describing the global security environment, DoD's strategic guidance singles out the global commons, the "areas beyond national jurisdiction that constitute the vital connective tissue of the international system."[7] After defining the importance of access in the global commons and the potential threats, the guidance says the United States will seek to assure access by "strengthening international norms of responsible behavior" and by maintaining military capabilities.[8]

Designing the overseas U.S. presence with the primary objective of safeguarding these domains, however, will not necessarily achieve the specific U.S. national security interests of defending the homeland against economic disruptions and terrorist threats, deterring aggressive action and military competition from hostile actors, and reassuring partners and allies against threats. See Appendix A for a more detailed discussion of the "global commons" as an approach to defining future global U.S. posture.

What is missing is an approach to defining the future overseas U.S. presence that focuses on achieving U.S. security interests globally, not just regionally, and with a specificity that is lacking in abstract discussions of the global commons.

---

[7] DoD, 2012, p. 3.

[8] DoD, 2012, p. 3

Analysis Framework

We took up the challenge and designed an analysis framework with four steps. The first step defines global U.S. security interests. Today's U.S. overseas military presence serves all these interests, and the question is whether and how it might do so in the future. Having defined them, it became clear that it would be necessary to specify the major threats to these interests and the countries in which they were located.

In the second step, we asked: What overseas U.S. presence is needed to achieve the U.S. security interests of deterring and dissuading North Korea, China, Iran, and potentially other adversaries; reassuring U.S. allies and partners in Europe, Asia, and the Middle East; and dissuading military competition and arms races with China and Iran? We found different perspectives on what will be needed.

This set the stage in the third step for our developing alternative global U.S. postures based on these different perspectives, or strategic views. By posture, we mean the network of overseas bases, forces, and activities (such as military exercises). These global postures are illustrative, as many combinations of perspectives could lead to a global posture. Using a database we constructed, we then described, again illustratively, the overseas U.S. Air Force (USAF) bases, forces, and activities that would be needed to implement each of the global postures.

Next, we compared the global postures, first in terms of their operational performance in different scenarios in Northeast Asia and Southwest Asia. We examined how well the global postures were able to support security interests that operate between and across regions—for example, to protect Americans from terrorist attacks and defend against economic disruptions, whether caused by hostile actors or natural disaster. We were also able to compare the five global postures in terms of their bases, active-duty personnel, and base operating costs.

Our analysis focused on the U.S. overseas military presence, not on U.S. military forces based in the United States. For global postures that decrease overseas presence, the analysis did not address what happens to the forces, i.e., whether they stay in the USAF force structure or not.

Using the global postures, we defined the strategic choices policymakers confront in defining a future overseas U.S. military presence. While there are no right or wrong choices, focusing on these makes it possible that, in the future, the U.S. presence will serve global U.S. security interests and not be based on other, unrelated considerations, such as costs or the political pressures of allies and congressional leaders.

Organization of This Monograph

Chapter Two outlines the path to our design of future U.S. global postures. It begins by identifying a set of seven discrete and enduring global national security interests and how these are likely in the future to be challenged in East Asia, Europe, and the Middle East. It defines different perspectives on what overseas U.S. presence is needed to achieve the major security interests of protecting U.S. allies and partners from threats from state adversaries, promoting U.S. influence in key regions, and dissuading arms races. Finally, five global postures emerge as we combine different perspectives.

Chapter Three compares the global postures in terms of their operational performance and, then, in how well they support the other global U.S. security interests of protecting Americans from terrorist attacks, restricting the flow of illegal trade and the proliferation of dangerous materials, ensuring the flow of commerce and key resources, and responding to humanitarian emergencies and regional conflicts. The chapter concludes with a comparison of the global postures in terms of the reductions that would occur in USAF bases, combat forces, active-duty personnel, and main base operating costs. Chapter Four concludes with a discussion of the strategic choices that policymakers face and how they might use our analytical framework in the future.

The monograph has three appendices. The first discusses the "global commons" as an approach to defining a future overseas U.S. presence. The second describes how we constructed the database of current U.S. bases overseas, which provided the basis for defining the characteristics of the global postures. The final appendix compares the global postures in terms of their overseas bases, missions, active-duty personnel, and main base operating costs.

CHAPTER TWO

Path to Defining Future Global U.S. Postures

Global U.S. Security Interests

In our approach to defining the future U.S. overseas presence, we focused directly on achieving specific U.S. security interests. Our review of recent U.S. strategy and defense documents, including the recent DoD strategic guidance, identified a list of seven discrete and enduring interests:

- protect U.S. allies and partners from state adversaries
- promote U.S. influence in key regions
- dissuade military competition and arms races
- protect Americans from terrorist attacks
- restrict the flow of illegal trade and the proliferation of dangerous materials
- ensure the flow of commerce and key resources
- respond to humanitarian emergencies and regional conflicts.[1]

In principle, each of these interests can be achieved through multiple means, of which U.S. forward military presence is just one. The United States might also undertake economic or other forms of nonmilitary assistance, pursue burden sharing with U.S. allies and partners, seek multilateral arrangements ranging from implicit agreements to codified

---

[1] See The White House, *National Security Strategy*, Washington, D.C., May 2010; DoD, 2012; DoD, *Nuclear Posture Review Report*, Washington, D.C., April 2010b; and Department of the Air Force, *United States Air Force Posture Statement*, Washington, D.C., February 2010.

international law, or rely on long-range or remotely deployed assets. We singled out the role of an overseas military presence while taking into account the possibility of changing current arrangements for burden sharing with U.S. allies and partners and also of relying more on military forces based in the United States.

While the seven interests above are global—the United States has an interest in dissuading military competition wherever it might arise, for example—the means it uses to achieve them must be responsive to the specific ways in which they are challenged in various parts of the world. An overseas presence that does not account for regional differences would be too broad, and therefore inefficient, likely leaving the United States well-prepared to manage threats in some areas but either overly or poorly prepared in others—through either a deficit of resources or use of counterproductive means.[2]

Threats in Asia are expanding beyond Northeast Asia to Southeast Asia, as China modernizes its military forces and seeks to assert its interests in the South China Sea. So, we focused on the region of East Asia to include these countries as a group: Japan, the Korean Peninsula, China, and Southeast Asia. We see no major threats to these security interests arising in the Western Hemisphere or in sub-Saharan Africa. Elsewhere, we view potential threats in Europe and Central Asia from Russia in its near abroad; in the Middle East from Iran, Syria, and non-state groups; and in Central and Southwest Asia from militant insurgents. Given the changing nature of these threats, we decided to focus on countries as a group across Europe, the Middle East, and Central and Southwest Asia, so as to be able to look at how the U.S. presence in Europe can respond to threats outside and at how the U.S. presence in the Middle East and Central Asia can respond to threats more broadly along the periphery of Europe and in Central and Southwest Asia.

---

[2] Rather than dissuading military competition, for example, U.S. forward military presence displaying U.S. conventional superiority might in fact drive weaker states (e.g., Iran) to pursue asymmetric or nonconventional capabilities and drive stronger states (e.g., China) to forgo conventional arms races in favor of investing in advanced space or cyber capabilities.

We focused on the first three U.S. security interests (and their specific regional goals) because they involve major threats to the United States and will likely be the main drivers in the design of the future U.S. overseas presence:

1. protect U.S. allies and partners from state adversaries
    – Asian allies from China and North Korea
    – Middle East partners from Iran, Syria, and violent nonstate groups
    – Asian and European partners from Russia
2. promote U.S. influence in key regions
    – re China in East Asia, Central Asia, and Africa
    – re Iran in the Middle East; Russia in its near abroad and in Central Asia
3. dissuade military competition and arms races
    – with China and North Korea
    – with Iran.

Starting this way, with the first three U.S. security interests, does not imply that the other global security interests of protecting Americans from terrorist attacks and defending against economic or other disruptions are not important or that these first three security interests would have priority for the United States in the future. In fact, protecting Americans from terrorist attacks is defined in the DoD strategic guidance as a mission for sizing future U.S. military forces. How well global postures accomplish these other interests will be discussed in the next chapter.

Perspectives on Global Presence Needed to Achieve U.S. Security Interests in East Asia, Europe, and the Middle East

Having specified U.S. security interests in East Asia in detail, we defined different perspectives on what future U.S. overseas military presence will be needed. To do this, we drew on the views of experts, both in academe and in the policy arena. More specifically, perspectives differ on whether and what types of overseas military presence can influence Chinese and North Korean decisions about the use of military force in a crisis or conflict, can provide reassurance to U.S. allies and partners, and can affect Chinese strategic and military planning. Perspectives can be based on historical influences on the behavior of different U.S. adversaries or on the views of regional experts, policymakers, etc. The perspectives cannot, however, be empirically tested because they involve views about how U.S. adversaries and friends will behave in the future. See Table 2.1 for the U.S. security interests in East Asia and the differing perspectives on the role of overseas U.S. military presence in achieving them.

In the same way, having specified U.S. security interests in the countries of Europe and the Middle East, we defined different perspectives on what future U.S. overseas military presence will be needed. To do this, we again drew on the views of experts, both in academe and in the policy arena. More specifically, is there still a role for U.S. presence in ensuring collective security in Europe? How important is U.S. presence onshore or offshore in the Middle East to influencing Iran's use of military force and in reassuring U.S. partners? See Table 2.2 for the U.S. security interests in Europe and the Middle East and the differing perspectives on the role of U.S. forward military presence in achieving them.

Perspectives Lead to Global Postures

Having defined the different perspectives on what overseas U.S. military presence is needed to achieve U.S. security interests in East Asia and across Europe and the Middle East, we next designed alternative global U.S. postures. These are illustrative, as many combinations of perspectives could lead to a global posture. Briefly, what follows for each of the global postures is a description of its strategic view, underlying rationale, and general characteristics in terms of bases, forces, and military activities, i.e., rotational deployments and military exercises. In our analysis, we did not consider what happens to the forces transi-

Table 2.1
Perspectives on Achieving U.S. Security Interests in East Asia

U.S. Security Interest	Differing Perspectives on What Foreign Military Presence Is Needed		
Deter and respond to Chinese threats to Taiwan and to other allies/partners across region	Need for U.S. presence to increase and expand geographically as Chinese threats increase across the region	Need to respond militarily to Chinese threats as they increase and expand geographically across region, but U.S. can share responsibility with Japan and S. Korea Need to increase U.S. presence in countries other than Japan and S. Korea to deter and respond to regional conflicts (South China Sea)	Depends on capabilities of U.S. military forces to surge and strike from U.S. in crises or conflicts, not specific levels of presence
Deter and respond to North Korean threats against South Korea and Japan	Need visible U.S. presence that involves robust conventional forces	Need U.S. presence but can depend on South Korea to take on more of the burden if the North Korean threat increases	Need U.S. military forces but does not depend on where these are located
Reassure U.S. allies and partners of credibility of U.S. security guarantees	Need for U.S. presence to increase and expand geographically to ensure stability and respond to China's military expansion	Achieved by some U.S. presence, specific numbers of bases or personnel are not necessary	Achieved by size and capabilities of U.S. military forces and their ability to respond to future threats, not specific levels of U.S. presence
Influence Chinese strategic and military planning	U.S. presence may be able to play limited role in dissuading Chinese military modernization	U.S. presence has little to do with Chinese military modernization	Reducing U.S. presence could moderate Chinese military modernization

Table 2.2
Perspectives on Achieving U.S. Security Interests in Countries Across Europe and the Middle East

U.S. Security Interest	Differing Perspectives on What Foreign Military Presence Is Needed		
Deter and respond to potential threats in Europe from Russia in countries along its periphery and reassure Eastern European allies and partners	Need U.S. presence to respond to potential threats to collective security and to reassure NATO allies and partners	Can rely on allies to assume responsibility for responding to potential threats to collective security	Threats to collective security have essentially disappeared and so need U.S. presence only to provide transit for supporting other U.S. interests
Deter and respond to potential threats and uses of force from Iran, Syria, and violent non-state groups against U.S. allies and partners and reassure U.S. partners in Middle East as to U.S. security guarantees	Need U.S. presence in Europe to deter and respond to conflict with Iran	Need U.S. presence in Europe to support U.S. interests in Middle East	Deterring and responding to Iran depends on size and capabilities of U.S. military forces, and their ability to respond to future threats quickly in the event of crises or conflict, not on specific levels of U.S. presence in Europe or GCC
	Need U.S. presence onshore and offshore in GCC states to be able quickly to defeat any attacks	Need limited U.S. presence onshore in GCC states to be able quickly to blunt small attacks	Allies and partners in Middle East capable of blunting coercive and other immediate Iranian threats
			Need only small U.S. permanent presence on shore augmented by naval forces and rotating air force deployments

tioned back to the United States, i.e., whether they are kept in the force structure or disbanded.

Global Posture 1: Long Range and Responsive

In this posture, the United States will rely largely on forces in the United States to respond to global crises and conflicts, keeping only a small global forward presence to reassure allies and partners.

This strategic view is based on these perspectives: Threats to collective security have essentially disappeared in Europe, and so U.S. forward presence is needed in Europe only to provide transit for supporting U.S. interests elsewhere. Deterring and responding to China, North Korea, and Iran depend on the size and capabilities of U.S. military forces and their ability to respond to threats quickly, not on specific levels of U.S. forward presence. Promoting U.S. influence also does not depend on U.S. forward presence, and U.S. allies and partners in the Middle East will be capable of blunting coercive and other immediate Iranian threats. Reducing the U.S. presence could also moderate the Chinese-American rivalry.[3]

Overseas presence in this global posture would be designed to provide the bases and mobility forces necessary for the United States to be able to surge forces from the United States and stage through bases in Europe, Japan, and the Republic of Korea (ROK). The contingency

---

[3]   While this global posture may appear to be similar to the "offshore balancing" strategy, it differs in a number of important ways. See Christopher Layne, "From Preponderance to Off-shore Balancing: America's Future Grand Strategy," *International Security*, Vol. 22, No. 1, Summer 1997, pp. 112–119. First, and most important, the United States does not disengage from the world or from supporting its allies. In a strategy of offshore balancing, however, the United States withdraws to the Western Hemisphere, turns over responsibility for maintaining the balance of power to regional states, and intervenes only if the states are unable to succeed on their own. Second, this global posture seeks to achieve current global U.S. security interests, while offshore balancing presupposes that American interests are narrowing to the point that the United States is interested only in defending its homeland and preventing the emergence of a Eurasian hegemon. For more on offshore balancing, see Christopher Layne, "Offshore Balancing Revisited," *Washington Quarterly*, Vol. 24, No. 2, Spring 2002, pp. 245–246; Barry R. Posen and Andrew L. Ross, "Competing Visions for U.S. Grand Strategy," *International Security*, Vol. 21, No. 3, Winter 1996/1997, pp. 7–14; and Eugene Gholz, Daryl G. Press, and Harvey M. Sapolsky, "Come Home, America: The Strategy of Restraint in the Face of Temptation," *International Security*, Vol. 21, No. 4, Spring 1997, pp. 5–48.

bases currently in Southeast Asia and Australia would be retained, and access to new, or what we will call "aspirational," bases in Malaysia would be sought. Bases in the Gulf Cooperation Council (GCC) states and Africa would not change but would become more austere, with some reduction in the permanent U.S. presence, consistent with the political environment and the need to provide reassurance to U.S. partners.

Ensuring access to these bases in future conflicts and building the necessary supporting infrastructure would be critical for this global posture. Preparing to respond from the United States would also require expanded exercises and, possibly, more temporary deployments of U.S. military forces globally. The United States would transfer all combat wings from Europe, South Korea, and all but one combat wing from Japan to U.S. territory. Mobility forces around the world would not change, except that those currently in the GCC states would transition home.

Global Posture 2: Forward in Asia

To influence future Chinese and North Korean military activities and to reassure U.S. allies and partners, the U.S. forward presence across Asia would need to increase in this global posture as Chinese and North Korean threats expand, but forces based primarily in the United States would be sufficient to deter and respond to threats in Europe and the Middle East. The U.S. presence in Asia may also be able to play a limited role in dissuading Chinese military modernization.

While U.S. overseas presence would not change in terms of planned U.S. bases and military forces in Japan and South Korea, the United States, to the extent that it becomes politically and fiscally possible, would expand its exercises and permanent presence in the Philippines, Thailand, Singapore, and Australia. Access to new or "aspirational" bases would be sought in Malaysia, Vietnam, and Indonesia to provide the United States with a more diversified presence across Southeast Asia, given China's expanding interests in the South China Sea.

The United States would depend primarily on military forces based in the United States to maintain stability in the Middle East, based on the perspectives that U.S. forward presence will not play a major role in influencing Iran's military actions and that U.S. partners in the GCC states will be able initially to blunt any Iranian attacks. The number of current U.S. bases in the GCC states and Africa will not change, but they would become more austere with some reduction in the permanent U.S. presence, consistent with the political and fiscal environment as well as the need to provide reassurance to U.S. partners.

Based on the perspective that threats to collective security have essentially disappeared in Europe, the U.S. overseas presence in Europe would be designed to provide the bases and forces necessary for the United States to be able to surge forces from the United States to respond to crises and conflicts in the Middle East and elsewhere.

In this global posture, the United States would increase its exercises with countries across East Asia and would be ready to increase its temporary presence through rotational deployments of air and naval forces, as the threats from China or North Korea increase. Critical also would be ensuring access to European staging bases in future conflicts and maintaining the necessary supporting infrastructure. Preparing to respond from the United States would also require expanded exercises and possibly more temporary deployments of military forces in the GCC states. The United States would transfer all combat forces in Europe and all mobility forces in the GCC states back to the United States.

Global Posture 3: Forward in the Middle East

The United States, in this global posture, would shift the focus of its future forward presence to responding to expanding threats and instabilities in the Middle East and would rely primarily on U.S.-based forces to respond to crises and conflicts in Asia.

This strategic view is based on the perspectives that the U.S. forward presence does not play a major role in influencing China's military activities or modernization and that threats to collective security in Europe have essentially disappeared.

So, the U.S. presence in Europe would decrease, and the remaining forces would be designed to deter and respond to threats from Iran, including the ability to surge aircraft into Europe for Iran contingencies. The resulting presence would also serve to reassure NATO allies and partners. Bases and forces would continue as today in the GCC states and Africa, with the aims of being able to blunt any attacks on U.S. partners quickly and of providing reassurance.

In Asia, the United States would, in future crises and conflicts rely primarily on forces from the United States to stage through bases in Japan and South Korea and through contingency bases currently in Southeast Asia and Australia. Access to a new base would be sought in Malaysia. Ensuring access to bases across East Asia in future conflicts and building the necessary supporting infrastructure would be critical in this global posture. Preparing to respond from the United States would also require expanded exercises in these countries and possibly more temporary deployments of U.S. military forces.

All combat forces in South Korea and one combat wing in Japan would transfer back to U.S. territory. Two combat wings would leave Europe. Overseas mobility forces would not change.

Global Posture 4: Shared with Allies and Diversified Globally

In this global posture, U.S. allies in Europe and Northeast Asia would assume primary responsibility for their own security, and the United States would shift the focus of its future forward presence to respond to expanding threats elsewhere, from China in Southeast Asia and from instabilities across the Middle East.

As in global posture 4, the U.S. presence in Europe would be designed to deter and respond to threats from Iran, although the resulting presence would also serve as a hedge against potential threats to collective security and would reassure NATO allies and partners. Bases would continue as today in the GCC states and Africa, with the permanent and rotational forces designed to blunt any attacks on U.S. partners quickly and to provide reassurance.

The U.S. presence in Japan and South Korea would decrease as these allies took on more responsibility for their own security. To respond to an expanding Chinese threat, the United States would seek new or "aspirational" bases in one or more countries in Southeast Asia, e.g., in Malaysia, Vietnam, and Indonesia. While keeping the size of

U.S. presence as today, exercises would also be expanded with Australia, the Philippines, Singapore, Thailand, the GCC states, and in Africa. Mobility forces would remain at bases in Europe, Japan, and the GCC, while two combat wings from Europe, one combat wing from Japan, and one combat wing from South Korea would transfer back to U.S. territory.

Global Posture 5: Forward Globally

In this posture, the United States would retain its forward presence in East Asia, Europe, and the Middle East and expand its future presence across Southeast Asia and the Middle East as the political and fiscal situations permit.

This strategic view is based on these perspectives: The United States would need to increase its presence in Asia to be able to deter and respond to Chinese and North Korean military expansion. A presence would be needed in the Middle East to be able to deter Iran and defeat any attacks quickly and in Europe as a hedge against potential threats to collective security and to reassure NATO allies and partners. These military forces in Europe would also be available for expeditionary contingencies with U.S. allies in Europe.

Within political constraints, the United States would seek to expand its permanent presence in the GCC states and Djibouti and to gain private agreements from the governments of Saudi Arabia and India to be able to operate from bases there in a crisis. All combat and mobility forces would be kept on current U.S. bases.

CHAPTER THREE

Comparison of Global Postures

This chapter compares the global postures in terms of their operational performance; ability to support the broader U.S. security interests; and base, personnel, and cost characteristics.

Operational Performance

Drawing on other RAND analyses, we looked at the operational performance of the bases in the global postures in different scenarios in Northeast Asia and Southwest Asia.[1] The scenarios were representative of the different U.S. global security interests described in Chapter Two. In Northeast Asia, the scenarios were Chinese conflicts with Taiwan, Japan, and Vietnam; North Korean attacks on South Korea; counterinsurgency in the Philippines; terrorist attacks in Indonesia; a humanitarian emergency in Sri Lanka (earthquake); and a government collapse in Burma. The scenarios in Southwest Asia were Iranian low-intensity attacks, internal instability in Yemen and Syria, a rescue operation in Pakistan, and piracy in the Northern Arabian Sea. The RAND analyses scored the effectiveness of individual bases in achieving specific military goals, e.g., F-16 orbits over Pakistan and MQ-9 orbits over Syria. The analyses assumed access to the bases in the scenarios and that the required air forces were able to operate from the bases. The analyses scored each of the bases (low, medium, or high) in

---

[1] Alan J. Vick and Jacob L. Heim, *Assessing U.S. Air Force Basing Options in East Asia*, Santa Monica, Calif.: RAND Corporation, MG-1204-AF, forthcoming. Our study did not undertake any operational analyses of the individual global postures.

three areas of performance: vulnerability, overflight access, and force structure capabilities.

We compiled these scores for each base in each global posture and then compared them. What emerged from these evaluations was that the global postures are similar in overall performance in these scenarios. Global postures scored "high" in some scenarios, e.g., in responding to Chinese conflicts over the Senkakus and Spratleys and to internal conflicts in Yemen and in Syria. They had similar constraints in certain scenarios: base vulnerability in Chinese conflicts with Taiwan and Vietnam; limitations in force structure in operations against Iran from European and GCC bases; and overflight access in responding to low-intensity conflict with Iran from European bases and in emergencies in Sri Lanka and in Burma. The global postures also relied on bases with uncertain access in certain scenarios, e.g., Philippine bases for counterinsurgency operations and GCC bases for operations against Iran. What this means is that steps will need to be taken in whichever global posture is chosen to remedy the deficiencies discovered in these operational evaluations.

The most serious constraint in the RAND scenario evaluations turned out to be the increasing vulnerability of U.S. bases to Chinese and Iranian missile attacks. Figure 3.1 shows the current projection for the Chinese and Iranian missile threats.

Each of the global postures has bases within Chinese and Iranian threat rings. As the threat increases and as these bases become increasingly vulnerable, incentives could arise for either side to use its forces early—to preempt—in a crisis, thereby undermining stability. The global postures differ, though, in the numbers of bases in these threat rings, with fewer in those that rely primarily on surging forces from the United States. Stability in these global postures could, however, be undermined in a different way, by pressuring an adversary to use its forces preemptively, before U.S. forces could arrive in the region.

Figure 3.1
Iranian and Chinese Missile Threat 2011

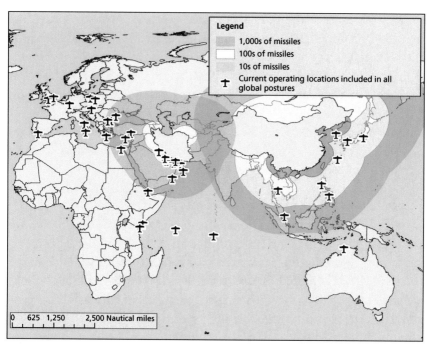

SOURCES: Jane's, "Strategic Weapon System, Iran," *Jane's Sentinel Security Assessment—The Gulf States*, September 16, 2011; Jane's, "Strategic Weapon Systems, China," *Jane's Sentinel Security Assessment—China and Northeast Asia*, January 17, 2011; Office of the Secretary of Defense, *Military and Security Developments Involving the People's Republic of China 2011*, Washington, D.C., 2011, p. 30; DoD, *Unclassified Report on the Military Power of Iran*, Washington, D.C., April 2010c, p. 11; and International Institute for Strategic Studies, *The Military Balance 2011*, London: IISS, March 2011, pp. 230–236, 309–311.

RAND *MG1211-3.1*

Global Postures Support Other U.S. Security Interests

For our analysis, we designed the alternative global postures to achieve the first three global U.S. security interests. Next, we asked how well these global postures would support the other global U.S. security interests—protecting Americans from terrorist attacks, restricting the flow of illegal trade and the proliferation of dangerous materials, ensuring the flow of commerce and key resources, and responding to humanitarian emergencies and regional conflicts.[2]

To do this, we started with a list of current U.S. bases that are common to each of the global postures.[3] Our goal was to provide a "snapshot" of how these bases would align with the potential demands in achieving each of these other global security interests. We were not able to go on to compare the global postures, because it is not clear that those with more bases (e.g., in Europe or Japan) would necessarily do any better. Obviously, more analysis would be required, especially in terms of the operational requirements and mix and numbers of forces, to actually design a global posture to achieve these other global security interests or to compare these global postures.

Protect Americans from Terrorist Attacks

Figure 3.2 illustrates the locations where al-Qaeda and its affiliates are operating and the current bases common to each of the global postures. The figure shows that these current bases span the al-Qaeda locations fairly well in the Middle East and Asia but that the United States could face challenges to its counterterrorism operations in Africa and in Central Asia.[4] So, acquiring the new or "aspirational" bases in Africa and India that are in some of the global postures could be very important, as would be keeping current bases in Afghanistan and Central Asia.

---

[2] In terms of sizing its military forces to include these other interests, the United States has historically tended to consider it being enough to have military forces sufficient for the first three, supplemented by some specific capabilities, such as special operations forces (SOF), in the case of protecting Americans from terrorist attacks. This changed after September 11, 2001, for counterterrorism and counterinsurgency missions. According to current strategic guidance, counterterrorism, but not counterinsurgency, is a mission for sizing U.S. military forces (DoD, 2012).

[3] See Appendix B for a list of the bases in common.

[4] In June 2012, the *Washington Post* reported that the United States had established a network of bases in Africa over the past five years for operations against al-Qaeda affiliates and other militant groups (Craig Whitlock, "U.S. Expands Secret Intelligence Operations in Africa," *Washington Post*, June 13, 2012).

Figure 3.2
Locations of Al-Qaeda and Affiliates

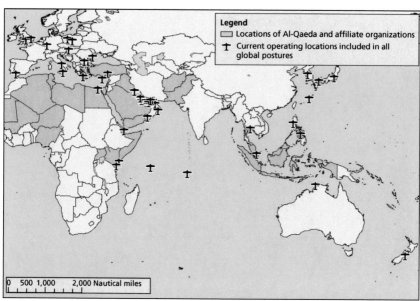

SOURCE: John Rollins, *Al Qaeda and Affiliates: Historical Perspective, Global Presence, and Implications for U.S. Policy*, Washington, D.C.: Congressional Research Service, CRS-R41070, February 5, 2010.
RAND *MG1211-3.2*

Restrict Flow of Illegal Trade and Ensure Flow of Commerce and Key Resources

Figure 3.3 illustrates the global shipping routes and the current bases common to each of the global postures. The figure shows a fairly good alignment between the bases and the major trade routes through Europe, Asia, and the Middle East. The United States could face more challenges in responding to threats along the secondary routes around the Horn of Africa and Australia.

Respond to Humanitarian Emergencies and Regional Conflicts

Figure 3.4 addresses how well the bases common to the global postures align with areas prone to natural disasters, focusing on hydrological (floods, cyclones, and landslides) and seismic disasters. The figure shows that they are really not that closely aligned.

Figure 3.3
Global Shipping Routes by Traffic Volume

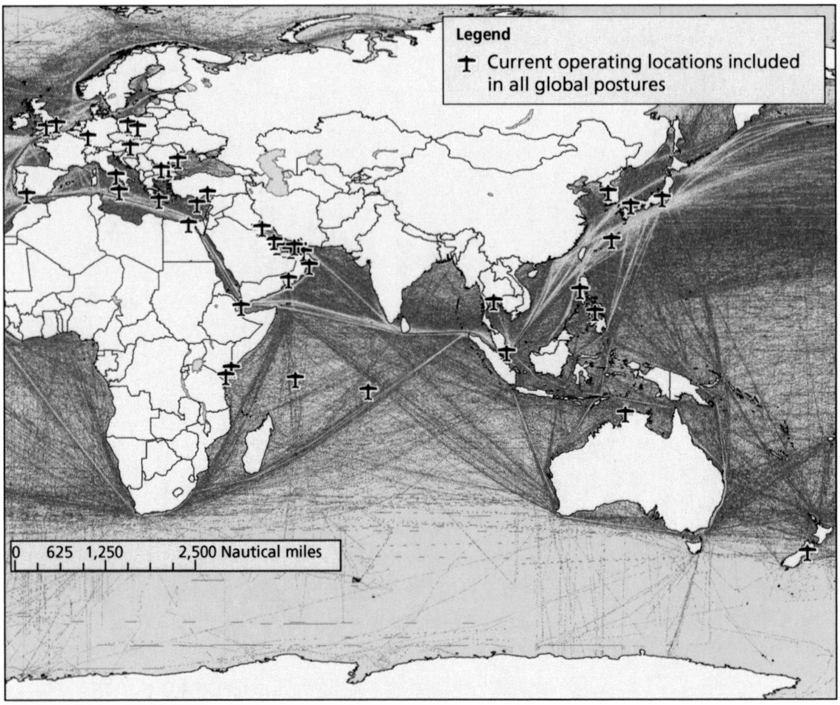

SOURCE: National Center for Ecological Analysis and Synthesis, A Global Map of Human Impacts to Marine Ecosystems: Commercial Activity (Shipping) Data Set, Goleta, Calif.: University of California, Santa Barbara, 2008.
RAND MG1211-3.3

Summary

As Figures 3.2–3.4 suggest, our analyses show similarities in how the postures support other U.S. global security interests even as they differ in their strategic views on the three major security interests, protecting U.S. allies and partners from state adversaries, promoting U.S. regional influence, and dissuading military competition and arms races. Adding the bases in the global postures 2–5 would not make much difference to this conclusion.

Figure 3.4
Risk of Mortality by Natural Disaster Type

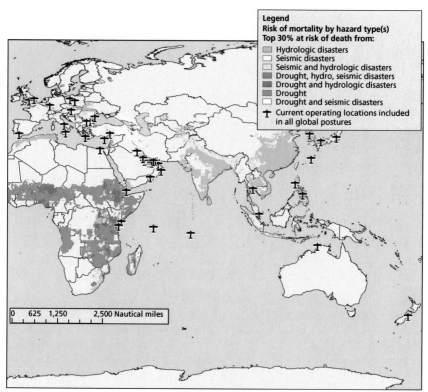

Legend
Risk of mortality by hazard type(s)
Top 30% at risk of death from:
- Hydrologic disasters
- Seismic disasters
- Seismic and hydrologic disasters
- Drought, hydro, seismic disasters
- Drought and hydrologic disasters
- Drought
- Drought and seismic disasters
- ✝ Current operating locations included in all global postures

SOURCE: Center for Hazards and Risk Research (CHRR) et al., *Global Multihazard Mortality Risks and Distribution*, V 1.0, Palisades, N.Y.: Columbia University, 2005.
RAND *MG1211-3.4*

Characteristics of Global Postures

We constructed a database of current overseas air bases (ABs) in East Asia, Europe, the Middle East, and Africa that are "enduring U.S. locations," i.e., where the United States intends to have long-term access whether troops are permanently stationed or rotationally deployed.[5]

---

[5] Appendix B describes the database, which was current as of the end of FY 2010. The sources for the database include the USAF website; unclassified information from DoD, *2011 U.S. Global Defense Posture Report to Congress*, Washington, D.C., May 2011b; the Global Security website; Air Mobility Command, *Air Mobility Command Global En Route*

We defined the USAF bases in each of the global postures, along with the types of forces (combat and mobility), the types of activities (permanent and rotational deployments). All the global postures in our illustrative designs include current U.S. and North Atlantic Treaty Organization (NATO) bases in Eastern Europe used by American forces, given their importance in continuing to build partnerships with these countries and their potential utility in military operations across the Middle East.[6] Working from the strategic view of the global posture, we then defined the other current overseas ABs that would be retained, turned over to a U.S. ally, or closed. We specified whether the base would remain as today, i.e., a main operating base (MOB), forward operating site (FOS), or cooperative security location (CSL), or would change its type.[7] See Appendix B.

Strategy White Paper, Scott Air Force Base: U.S. Air Force, July 14, 2010; Commission on Review of the Overseas Military Facilities Structure of the United States, *Commission on Review of the Overseas Military Facilities Structure of the United States Report*, May 9, 2005; DoD, *Base Structure Report Fiscal Year 2011 Baseline*, Washington, D.C., 2011a; Paul Koring and Borzou Daragahi, "The Canadian Forces Base at Camp Mirage Is Having Trouble Staying Under Wraps," *The Globe and Mail*, May 21, 2005; Kenneth Katzman, *Bahrain: Reform, Security, and U.S. Policy*, Washington, D.C.: Congressional Research Service, January 5, 2011a; Kenneth Katzman, *The United Arab Emirates (UAE): Issues for U.S. Policy*, Washington, D.C.: Congressional Research Service, March 10, 2011b; Kenneth Katzman, *Oman: Reform, Security, and U.S. Policy*, Washington, D.C.: Congressional Research Service, April 13, 2011c; Kenneth Katzman, *Kuwait: Security, Reform, and U.S. Policy*, Washington, D.C.: Congressional Research Service, April 26, 2011d; Christopher M. Blanchard, *Qatar: Background and U.S. Relations*, Washington, D.C.: Congressional Research Service, May 16, 2011.

[6]   In each of the global postures, U.S. Navy and Marine Corps bases are retained where there is an Air Force presence: Diego Garcia, Iwakuni in Japan, Souda Bay in Greece, Sigonella and Naples in Italy, Rota in Spain, and Muharraq/Manama in Bahrain. A few other bases were included in each of the global postures: in Cyprus, New Zealand, Kenya (Mombassa International Airport and Manda Bay), Seychelles, UAE, and Royal Air Force (RAF) Fairford in the United Kingdom.

[7]   An MOB contains a sizable and permanent U.S. military presence that often includes families and typically provides a high standard of living. An FOS regularly hosts rotational American military units but has only a small permanent U.S. military caretaker presence. A CSL contains no permanent U.S. presence; instead, rotational U.S. forces occasionally use it for training and during contingencies. (DoD, 2011b; National Defense University, 2011 Worldwide Posture Conference, June 14–15, 2011.)

None of the new, "aspirational," bases that we introduced into the global postures are included in these illustrative designs, neither are bases in Afghanistan and Central Asia, given the uncertainties about whether these bases will be available in the future.[8]

The global postures differ in their strategic view as well as potential reductions in overseas presence. See Table 3.1. Appendix C provides the supporting analyses and references for this table. As described in Appendixes B and C, the USAF overseas presence at the end FY 2010 consisted of a total of 60 bases; seven overseas wings of combat forces; and 46,700 overseas active-duty personnel. The annual operating costs for the MOBs were $7.9 billion. The reductions in the global postures shown in Table 3.1 are from these totals.

Reductions in overseas annual MOB operating costs show a range, with the lower figure presuming that the bases are closed but that the weapons systems and personnel are retained and operated at a different location. The higher figure presumes that the bases are closed and that the weapons and personnel are cut from the USAF force structure. The costs for other bases in the global postures are not included, including potential investments to be able to operate in these and new bases. The considerable costs of closing bases and moving military forces and personnel to U.S. locations are also not included.

---

[8] Our analytical approach could be applied to bases in Afghanistan and Central Asia as the security environment in the region evolves.

Table 3.1
Characteristics of Global Postures

Global Posture	Strategic View	Overseas Presence[a]			
		Bases	Combat Forces	Active Duty Personnel	Annual Operating Costs ($B)
1. Long-Range and Responsive	U.S. will rely primarily on U.S.-based forces to respond to global crises and conflicts, keeping only a small global forward presence to reassure allies and partners.	Close 15	Reduce 3 wings in Europe, 1 wing in Japan, 2 wings in ROK	Reduce 23,800	Minus 1.5–3.8
2. Forward in Asia	U.S. forward presence across Asia will need to increase as Chinese and N. Korean threats expand, but forces based primarily in U.S. will be sufficient to deter and respond to threats in Europe and in the Middle East.	Close 8	Reduce 3 wings in Europe	Reduce 13,300	Minus 0.9–2.3
3. Forward in Middle East	U.S. will shift the focus of future forward presence to responding to expanding threats and instabilities in the Middle East and rely on U.S.-based forces to respond to crises and conflicts in Asia.	Close 13	Reduce 2 wings in Europe, 1 wing in Japan, 2 wings in ROK	Reduce 19,900	Minus 1.4–3.2
4. Shared with Allies and Diversified Globally	U.S. allies will assume primary responsibility for their security in Europe and N.E. Asia, and U.S. will shift focus of future forward presence to responding to threats in the Middle East and in Southeast Asia.	Close 11	Reduce 2 wings in Europe, 1 wing in Japan, 1 wing in ROK	Reduce 14,900	Minus 0.7–1.8
5. Forward Globally	U.S. forward presence will expand in Asia and in the Middle East as threats and instabilities increase and will change little in Europe.	No Change	No Change	No Change	No Change

[a] Actual reductions would depend on which bases were closed. Overseas active-duty personnel are as of the end of FY 2010. Operating costs are for MOBs; the lower figure presumes weapon systems and personnel are retained and the higher figure that they are cut from the USAF force structure. Costs for other bases are not included, such as potential investments to be able to operate in these and new bases.

CHAPTER FOUR

Strategic Choices: Overseas U.S. Military Presence

The overseas U.S. military presence is changing. Reductions are occurring as a result of the drawdown from Iraq and Afghanistan. What, if any, military bases and forces will remain in Afghanistan and Central Asia remains uncertain, given the complexity of the political situations in these countries. Pressures on defense spending have led to cuts in Army and USAF force structure, and the services have chosen to reduce some of their presence in Europe. The rest of the bases and military forces in the global U.S. posture are primarily those left at the end of past U.S. wars. Even the call in the recent DoD strategic guidance to "re-balance to the Asia-Pacific" will lead to only small changes and these over some years, as Marines deploy to Australia and talks proceed to increase joint military exercises with Singapore and the Philippines.

One reason for the resistance to change is that reductions in overseas presence yield only relatively small cost savings, and when cutting the defense budget, reductions tend to focus on manpower, force structure, and acquisition programs. When the reductions are in force structure, they could, but will not necessarily, come from overseas. This is the case because overseas presence often becomes tied to the overall foreign policy relationship the United States has with countries. So pressures can also arise for keeping bases and military forces even when the military reasons disappear. At the same time, countervailing domestic pressures are appearing from congressmen opposed to closing military bases in their districts and from those in Japan and South Korea living in close proximity to U.S. military bases.

Perhaps the most important reason for how little overseas U.S. military presence has changed is the lack of consensus on what is needed or how to link the number of bases and military forces overseas to specific U.S. global security interests. Perspectives differ on what overseas presence is needed to deter and respond to state adversaries, to reassure U.S. partners and allies, and to blunt arms races, as do views on whether a greater or different overseas U.S. presence is needed to achieve transnational U.S. security interests (counterterrorism, nonproliferation, humanitarian responses). Rarely are these perspectives articulated or are the views discussed in policy circles or in the public debate.

For this monograph, we designed an analytical approach that started with U.S. global security interests and recognized that policymakers hold these different perspectives. We then designed global postures based on alternative strategic views and illustrated each of these in terms of their USAF bases, combat forces, active-duty personnel, and operating costs. What emerged from our analyses are the critical strategic choices that policymakers need to address and the public needs to debate as they consider future overseas U.S. military presence.

The first strategic choice is for the United States to decide whether its overseas military presence can be reduced and diversified because its allies in Europe and Northeast Asia have the ability economically and militarily to assume primary responsibility for their own security. Such a choice could involve, for example, the United States reducing bases and combat forces in the United Kingdom, Germany, Japan, and South Korea. The remaining permanent U.S. overseas presence would provide the bases and military forces for immediate responses to future threats and to reassure U.S. allies and partners. The United States would then have the flexibility to expand its rotational presence across Southeast and Southwest Asia if threats were to increase or if partners were to call for reassurance.

If relying more on U.S. allies seems risky, given their reliance on nonmilitary strategies for responding to potential military threats and their political and economic constraints on defense spending, the United States would face other strategic choices with respect to its future overseas military presence. One is whether it is time for the

United States to rely primarily on U.S.-based forces to respond to global crises and conflicts, keeping only a small global forward presence to reassure allies and partners. Such a choice would be based on the perspective that deterring and responding to China, North Korea, and Iran in the future will depend not on overseas presence but rather on the ability of U.S. military forces at home to surge into the regions in the event of crises or conflicts. This would be the case for reassuring U.S. allies and partners as well. Such a choice would involve the United States relying on mobility forces and bases overseas, plus only a few combat forces, and on its ability to access bases more globally were threats from China and Iran to expand. Transitioning U.S. military forces to the United States would have the advantage of reducing their vulnerability to expanding missile threats.

Choosing to reduce the U.S. overseas military presence does not make sense if the perspective is that overseas U.S. presence plays an important role in deterring and responding to one or more of the threats from China, North Korea, and Iran and also in reassuring U.S. allies and partners. The strategic choice that then arises is whether the United States should maintain its global posture essentially as today and prepare to increase its overseas presence in Southeast and Southwest Asia if threats expand. Keeping existing bases would have the advantage of reducing the risks associated with not being able to return to bases after giving them up.

Such a robust global posture could, however, become too expensive or politically problematic in some countries. So the final strategic choice is whether the United States should focus its overseas U.S. presence more on Asia (because of the need to influence China's expanding military activities) or on the Middle East (because of the threats to stability and the flow of oil from a potentially nuclear-armed Iran). Choosing to emphasize Asia would involve keeping planned bases and military forces in Japan and South Korea, then expanding rotational deployments and exercises to the extent they become politically feasible with countries in Southeast Asia. Choosing to emphasize the Middle East would have the United States rely more on surging military forces from the United States for contingencies in Asia and keeping bases in the GCC states and Africa to be able to blunt any attacks on U.S.

partners quickly and to provide reassurance. In each of these cases, the choice would involve reorienting the focus of U.S. military forces in Europe to be able to surge forces from the United States to respond to crises and conflicts in the region where U.S. presence was reduced.

There is no one right strategic choice, but in our view, those involved in debates on the future U.S. global posture need to make explicit their implicit underlying perspectives on what role overseas military presence can play in achieving U.S. global security interests and then make decisions based on this menu of strategic choices. This would make it possible that decisions on the future U.S. overseas military presence can be based on agreement on how well it serves U.S. global security interests and not on other, unrelated considerations, as is often the case today.

Protecting The Global Commons: Confusing Means With Ends

Transnational threats to what are called the global commons—the air, sea, and space domains available for the use of all international actors but that none owns—have become a subject of interest to observers and practitioners of U.S. defense policy. In an influential 2009 article, former Under Secretary of Defense for Policy Michele Flournoy and a strategist in the Office of the Secretary of Defense, Shawn Brimley, identified the stability of the commons as not simply being important to national security but rather as being "central to the maintenance of U.S. power and influence."[1] The most recent round of U.S. strategy statements is attentive to the global commons, with the National Security Strategy identifying their "safeguarding" as a U.S. priority,[2] the Quadrennial Defense Review codifying DoD's commitment to maintaining secure access to this "connective tissue of the international system,"[3] and the strategic guidance focusing on the importance of access in the global commons and stating that the United States will seek to assure access by strengthening international norms of responsible behavior and by maintaining military capabilities.[4] As these documents demonstrate, the objectives of safeguarding the global commons

---

[1] Michele Flournoy and Shawn Brimley, "The Contested Commons," *Proceedings*, Vol. 135, July 2009.

[2] The White House, *National Security Strategy*, Washington, D.C., May 2010, p. 49.

[3] DoD, *Quadrennial Defense Review Report,* Washington, D.C., February 2010a.

[4] DoD, 2012, p. 3.

and of maintaining secure U.S. access to them often are used interchangeably but in fact represent different understandings of U.S. interests in the commons and, as a result, have different implications for the future U.S. global posture.

The first understanding contends that ensuring the security and stability of the global commons not only allows the United States its own freedom of action but, equally important, supports an inclusive international system that propagates "Western values including individual freedom, democracy, and liberty."[5] Stewardship of the commons, therefore, is itself a national security interest—an end to be pursued—and so the safeguarding of these domains is a necessary objective of U.S. defense policy. Most who subscribe to this position recommend a defense strategy in which security cooperation and international agreements figure just as prominently as forward military presence, if not more so.[6] Emphasis on these means is a product both of the size and scope of the commons and of the nature of competition within them: It is, over time, cheaper and easier for some hostile actors to acquire long-range missiles and antiship, antiarmor, antisatellite, and other disruptive weapons and technologies than it is for the United States to defend its forward-based assets and forces against them. Indeed, the increasing vulnerability of forward military presence to antiaccess threats is often cited as the most important harbinger of coming instability in the commons. It would thus be surprising for forward presence to be presented as the primary hedge against it.

The second approach to U.S. interests in the global commons views the openness of these domains not as an end but, rather, as a

---

[5] Flournoy and Brimley, 2009.

[6] Flournoy and Brimley, 2009; The White House, 2010; Abraham M. Denmark and James Mulvenon, eds., *Contested Commons: The Future of American Power in a Multipolar World*, Washington, D.C.: Center for a New American Security, January 2010, p. 67; Gary Hart, *Under the Eagle's Wing: A National Security Strategy of the United States for 2009*, Golden, Colo.: Fulcrum Publishing, 2008; and Michael Horowitz, *A Common Future? NATO and the Protection of the Commons*, Chicago, Ill.: The Chicago Council on Global Affairs, Transatlantic Paper Series No. 3, October 2010.

means to an end.[7] This perspective asserts that the United States need concern itself primarily with ensuring its own secure use of space and of the specific air and sea geographies necessary to fuel its economy, defend the homeland, deter hostile actors, and reassure allies. Pursuit of these objectives may also create stability in the commons that is to the benefit of others, but this is a positive result and not a purpose. In many regards, this approach to the commons is an application of new language to old concepts. That the United States must address the threats from state competitors, hostile nonstate actors, failed states, and natural disasters as they arise in the traditional mediums of air and sea and in the new medium of space is the usual business of international politics—of seeking to be stronger, faster, and smarter than potential rivals, for as long as possible.[8]

Designing a force posture for the commons as an end also does not ensure that the United States can achieve its other interests. Because safeguarding strategies are likely to rely heavily on security cooperation and international agreements and because the force implications of mounting a defense of the space domain are currently limited, the forward presence included in these approaches is unlikely to be as sizeable as and/or operationally equivalent to that required to achieve these other objectives. Designing a force posture for the commons as a means, in contrast, positions the United States to manage the most serious and direct challenges to U.S. interests as they operate in and across the commons' domains and gives it the capability and flexibility of determining whether, and how, to respond to other disruptions to the commons as they arise.

Keeping the global commons—the air, sea, and space domains— available for use by all yet owned by none is fundamental to the prosperity and security of the United States. However, the concept of safeguarding the global commons is not a useful construct for force

---

[7]   Barry R. Posen, "Command of the Commons: The Military Foundation of U.S. Hegemony," *International Security*, Vol. 28, No. 1, 2003, pp. 5–46.

[8]   See, for example, Kenneth Waltz, *Theory of International Politics*, New York: McGraw Hill, 1979; John J. Mearsheimer, *The Tragedy of Great Power Politics*, New York: W.W. Norton & Company, 2001; and Dale C. Copeland, *The Origins of Major War*, Ithaca, N.Y.: Cornell University Press, 2000.

planning and designing U.S. overseas presence. Rather, as argued in this report, U.S. overseas presence should be designed to secure global U.S. national security interests: defending the homeland against economic disruptions and terrorist threats; deterring aggressive action and military competition from hostile actors; and reassuring partners and allies against threats.

Database of Current U.S. Bases Overseas

We constructed a database of East Asian, European, Middle Eastern, and African airfields that the USAF currently uses that are "enduring U.S. locations," i.e., places to which the U.S. intends to maintain long-term access, whether it deploys forces on a permanent or rotational basis.[1] Since the database includes only unclassified information, some bases involved in sensitive operations may not be included.[2]

Each base is categorized as a MOB, FOS, or CSL.[3] Additionally, the database identifies all the bases that are currently a part of the Air Mobility Command (AMC) en route infrastructure.[4] Active-duty personnel permanently assigned to the base are also in the database and drawn from the USAF Personnel Center's Interactive Demographic Analysis System database. These personnel figures are current as of the end of FY 2010.

---

[1] This database was current as of the end of FY 2010. The sources for the database include the USAF website; unclassified information from the DoD, 2011b; the Global Security website; Air Mobility Command, 2010; Commission on Review of the Overseas Military Facilities Structure of the United States, 2005; DoD, 2011a; Koring and Daragahi, 2005; Katzman, 2011a, 2011b, 2011c, 2011d; Blanchard, 2011.

[2] Other bases were excluded from the database for other reasons: St. Helena Airfield, Klein Brogel, Buechel, Thule, San Vito dei Normanni, and RAF Alconbury. In each case, either the airfields had been shut down, the United States maintains only munitions support units, or the base was outside the geographic scope of the study.

[3] To categorize the bases, we consistently applied the definitions outlined in the earlier footnote to each of the installations. Our categorization, however, does not always match up with the way that DoD classifies these bases.

[4] As defined in AMC, 2010.

Figure B.1 shows a map of current USAF bases in each of the global postures, and Table B.1 lists these bases, their type, and their forces.

See Table B.2 for a list of current USAF bases that are not in all the global postures, including which bases are in which of the global postures.

Figure B.1
Current USAF Bases Common to All Global Postures

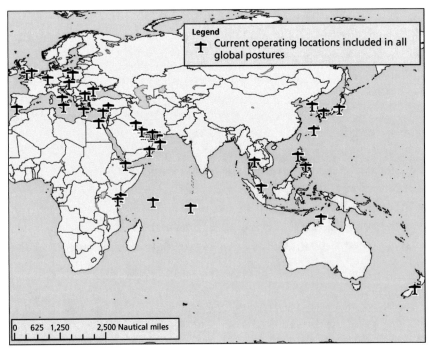

Table B.1
Airfields Presently Used by USAF Common to All Global Postures

Country	Base	Type	Forces
Australia	RAAF Darwin	CSL	Training location Rotational bombers and tankers
Japan	Yokota AB	MOB	374th Mobility Wing (C-130, C-12, UH-1) U.S. Forces Japan 5th Air Force
Japan (Okinawa)	Kadena AB	MOB	AMC, 18th Wing, 2 squadrons F-15C/D; KC-135s, E-3s, HH-60s, P-3s, MC-130, PAC-3, ammo storage
Philippines	Clark AB	CSL	AMC, training
Philippines	Mactan AB	CSL	Rotational P-3s
Singapore	Paya Labar AB	FOS	AMC, humanitarian assistance and disaster relief, logistics support
Thailand	U-Tapao	CSL	AMC, humanitarian assistance and disaster relief
Bulgaria	Bezmer AB	CSL	JTF-E Rotational fighters and lift, Training
Bulgaria	Graf Ignatievo AB	CSL	JTF-E Rotational fighters and lift, Training
Germany	Ramstein AB	MOB	86th Mobility Wing (C-130, C-20, C-21, C-40) U.S. Air Forces in Europe Headquarters 3rd Air Force Headquarters 17th Air Force Headquarters 435th Air Base Wing (support) Headquarters Allied Air Command NATO Continuous Presence aircraft: C-5, C-17, KC-135, KC-10
Hungary	Papa AB	MOB	NATO Heavy Airlift Wing (C-17s)
Poland	Krzesiny AB	CSL	Training
Poland	Lask AB	CSL	Training
Romania	Mihail Kogalniceanu AB	FOS	JTF-E Rotational fighters and lift, Training
Turkey	Incirlik	MOB	39th Air Base Wing (support) Continuous presence aircraft C-5, C-17, C-130, KC-135, KC-10

Table B.1—Continued

Country	Base	Type	Forces
United Kingdom	RAF Mildenhall	MOB	100th Air Refueling Wing (KC-135s) 95th Reconnaissance Squadron (RC-135s, OC-135s) 352nd Special Ops Groups (MC-130P, UC-12M, MC-130H) 3rd Air Force 727th AMC Squadron (support)
Bahrain	Isa AB	CSL	
Djibouti	Camp Lemonier	FOS	AMC, Headquarters JTF-HOA SOF, UAVs
Egypt	Cairo West	CSL	AMC Staging and refueling
Kuwait	Ali Al Salem AB	FOS	386th Air Expeditionary Wing Tactical Mobility (C-130, EC-130) Contingency Aeromedical Staging Facility
Kuwait	Al Mubarak/ Kuwait International Airport	CSL	AMC
Kuwait	Al Jaber AB	CSL	
Oman	Masirah Island AB	CSL	Prepositioning U.S. Navy aircraft maintenance Staging
Oman	Al Musanah	CSL	Prepositioning Staging
Oman	Thumrait AB	CSL	Prepositioning
Qatar	Al Udeid AB	MOB	Combat Air Operations Center U.S. Central Command 379th Air Expeditionary Wing (90 aircraft: B-1Bs, KC-135s, E-8C, RC-135, P-3s, C-17s, C-130s) Prepositioning
UAE	Al Dhafra AB	FOS	380th Air Expeditionary Wing (KC-10, E-3, U-2, RQ-4)
UAE	Fujairah AB and Port	CSL	Aerial port of debarkation Naval support

NOTE: Included in the global postures, but not shown in this table are U.S. Navy and Marine Corps bases having an Air Force presence (Diego Garcia, Iwakuni in Japan, Souda Bay in Greece, Sigonella and Naples in Italy, Rota in Spain, and Muharraq/ Manama in Bahrain) and current bases in Cyprus, New Zealand, Kenya (Mombassa International Airport and Manda Bay), Seychelles, UAE, and RAF Fairford in the United Kingdom.

Table B.2
Air Fields Presently Used by USAF in Some Global Postures

Country	Base	Type	Forces	Posture Number 1	2	3	4	5
Australia	RAAF Richmond	CSL	AMC		X			X
Japan	Misawa AB	MOB	AMC 35th Fighter Wing 2 squadrons F-16CJs NAF Misawa Shelters P-3 JTAGS-G		X		X	X
Japan	Shimoji AB	CSL	Mobility refueling		X			X
ROK	Kunsan AB	MOB	8th Fighter Wing 35th Fighter Squadron (F-16C/Ds) 80th Fighter Squadron (F-16C/Ds) Alpha Battery 2nd Battalion of 1st Air Defense Artillery (Patriot missiles)		X			
ROK	Osan AB	MOB	51st Fighter Wing 35th Fighter Squadron (A-10s) 36th Fighter Squadron (F-16C/Ds) 7th Air Force 731st Air Mobility Squadron (support)		X		X	X
ROK	Suwon AB	FOS	1st Battalion 43rd Air Defense Artillery Regiment (Patriot missiles) Surge location		X			X
ROK	Kwangju AB	FOS	Prepositioning Surge location		X			X

Table B.2—Continued

Country	Base	Type	Forces	1	2	3	4	5
						Posture Number		
ROK	K-2 AB	FOS	Surge location 607th Materiel Maintenance Squadron		X			X
Belgium	Florennes AB	FOS						X
Denmark	Karup AB	FOS						X
Germany	Spangdahlem AB	MOB	52nd Fighter Wing 1 squadron A-10s 2 squadrons F-16CMs Continuous presence aircraft: C-5, C-17, KC-135, KC-10					X
Germany	Geilenkirchen AB	MOB	NATO E-3A Component			X	X	X
Italy	Aviano	MOB	AMC 34th Fighter Wing 2 squadrons F-16CMs			X	X	X
Portugal (Azores)	Lajes Field	MOB	65th Air Base Wing (support) Defense Logistics Agency Fuel Depot	X	X			X
Spain	Moron AB	FOS	AMC NATO refueling Prepositioning (U.S. Air Forces in Europe munitions)	X	X			X
Turkey	Izmir Air Station	FOS	425 Air Base Squadron (support)			X	X	X
Turkey	Batman AB	CSL	Inactive			X	X	X
UK	RAF Lakenheath	MOB	48th Fighter Wing: 2 squadrons F-15Es 1 squadron F-15C 1 squadron HH-60			X	X	X

Comparison of Global Postures

Using the database described in Appendix B, we compared the five global postures in terms of their USAF missions and permanent and rotational overseas presence. Next, using other USAF databases, we compared the five global postures in terms of their overseas active-duty personnel and annual MOB operating costs at the end of FY 2010.

The USAF overseas presence at the end FY 2010 consisted of a total of 60 bases; seven overseas wings of combat forces; and 46,700 overseas active-duty personnel; the annual operating costs for the MOBs were $7.9 billion.

Missions at Bases in Global Postures

Overseas U.S. bases have different military missions that can be defined in different ways. For our analysis, we grouped the military missions into four categories: combat; mobility; training and other support; and intelligence, surveillance, and reconnaissance. We identified the primary mission for each base. Primary missions typically involve the majority of the USAF forces or the largest USAF unit at the base, while smaller units and rotational forces carry out the secondary missions. Figure C.1 shows the current bases in each of the global postures with their types of primary missions. Differences exist in the global postures for each of the missions.

These missions can be undertaken with permanently deployed forces at the base or with forces that rotate to the bases and return to the United States. The database described in Appendix B also catego-

Figure C.1
Global Postures: Primary Air Force Missions, 2010

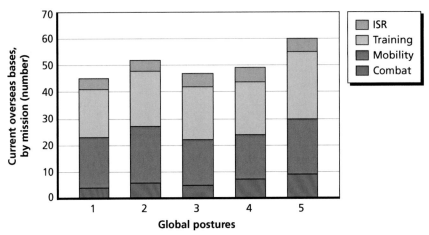

RAND *MG1211-C.1*

rizes each of the missions at each base as permanent or rotational. If the forces that perform a mission are permanently assigned to the base or continuously present at the location, it is designated as permanent. By contrast, when personnel and aircraft are only intermittently present, the mission is identified as rotational. Figure C.2 shows the current bases in each of the global postures and whether these house permanent or rotational forces in carrying out their primary missions.

Global Postures: Personnel and Base Operating Costs

We next compared the global postures in terms of permanently stationed overseas active-duty personnel in 2010 at current bases in each of the global postures (see Figure C.3).

The global postures differ as well in the annual MOB operating costs (see Figure C.4). The costs in 2010 reflect the direct and indirect costs at each of these bases. Direct costs are those directly associated with a weapon system or program. For an aircraft system, they would include all the assigned crew, maintenance, and other personnel and the fuel, material costs, and other services needed to operate and main-

Figure C.2
Global Postures: Permanent or Rotational Presence, 2010

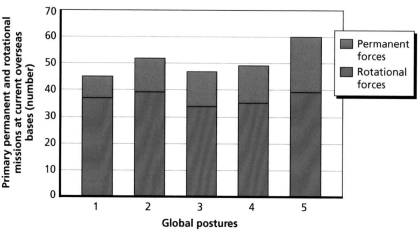

RAND MG1211-C.2

Figure C.3
Global Postures: USAF Active-Duty Personnel Overseas, 2010

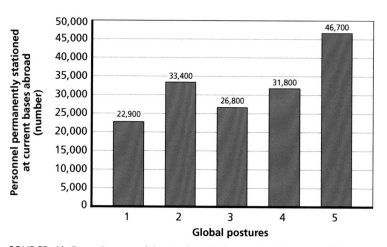

SOURCE: Air Force Personnel Center (AFPC), Interactive Demographic
Analysis System (IDEAS) database, Randolph Air Force Base, Tex., 2010.
RAND MG1211-C.3

Figure C.4
Global Postures: Annual Operating Costs at Current USAF Main Operating Bases, 2010

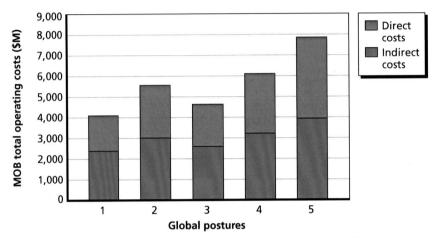

SOURCE: Secretary of the Air Force (SAF/FMFT), Air Force Total Ownership Cost (AFTOC), database, not available to the general public.
RAND *MG1211-C.4*

tain the system. Indirect costs are activities not directly attributable to a weapon system or program but to the infrastructure of an installation. Indirect costs include utilities, services, and personnel costs associated with base operating support, for example. The costs for other bases in the global postures are not included, including potential investments to be able to operate in these and new bases.

Closing a base or installation would eliminate the indirect costs, assuming that the personnel at that base or installation were reassigned. What happens with respect to the direct costs would depend on what happened to the weapon system and the personnel assigned to it. So, if the weapon system and personnel were retained and operated at a different location, the direct costs would simply be incurred at the different location.

Bibliography

Air Force Personnel Center (AFPC), Interactive Demographic Analysis System (IDEAS) database, Randolph Air Force Base, Tex., 2010.

Air Mobility Command, *Air Mobility Command Global En Route Strategy White Paper*, Scott Air Force Base: U.S. Air Force, July 14, 2010.

Blanchard, Christopher M., *Qatar: Background and U.S. Relations*, Washington, D.C.: Congressional Research Service, May 16, 2011.

Bumiller, Elisabeth, and Thom Shanker, "Defense Budget Cuts Would Limit Raises and Close Bases," *New York Times*, January 26, 2012. As of April 13, 2012: http://www.nytimes.com/2012/01/27/us/pentagon-proposes-limiting-raises-and-closing-bases-to-cut-budget.html?

Center for Hazards and Risk Research (CHRR), Columbia University; Center for International Earth Science Information Network (CIESIN), Columbia University; International Bank for Reconstruction and Development/The World Bank, *Global Multihazard Mortality Risks and Distribution*, V 1.0, Palisades, N.Y.: Columbia University, 2005.

Commission on Review of the Overseas Military Facilities Structure of the United States, *Commission on Review of the Overseas Military Facilities Structure of the United States Report*, May 9, 2005.

Copeland, Dale C., *The Origins of Major War*, Ithaca, N.Y.: Cornell University Press, 2000.

Denmark, Abraham M., and James Mulvenon, eds., *Contested Commons: The Future of American Power in a Multipolar World*, Washington, D.C.: Center for a New American Security, January 2010. As of December 1, 2011: http://www.cnas.org/files/documents/publications/CNAS%20Contested%20Commons_1.pdf

Department of the Air Force, *United States Air Force Posture Statement*, Washington, D.C., February 2010.

DoD—See U.S. Department of Defense.

Flournoy, Michele, and Shawn Brimley, "The Contested Commons," *Proceedings*, Vol. 135, July 2009, p. 277.

Gholz, Eugene, Daryl G. Press, and Harvey M. Sapolsky, "Come Home, America: The Strategy of Restraint in the Face of Temptation," *International Security*, Vol. 21, No. 4, Spring 1997, pp. 5–48.

Global Security, website, undated. As of May 14, 2012:
http://www.globalsecurity.org

Hart, Gary, *Under the Eagle's Wing: A National Security Strategy of the United States for 2009*, Golden, Colo.: Fulcrum Publishing, 2008.

Horowitz, Michael, *A Common Future? NATO and the Protection of the Commons*, Chicago, Ill.: The Chicago Council on Global Affairs, Transatlantic Paper Series No. 3, October 2010. As of December 1, 2011:
http://www.thechicagocouncil.org/userfiles/file/task%20force%20reports/Trans-Atlantic_Papers_3-Horowitz.pdf

International Institute for Strategic Studies, *The Military Balance 2011*, London: IISS, March 2011.

Jane's, "Strategic Weapon System, Iran," *Jane's Sentinel Security Assessment—The Gulf States*, September 16, 2011.

———, "Strategic Weapon Systems, China," *Jane's Sentinel Security Assessment—China and Northeast Asia*, January 17, 2011.

Katzman, Kenneth, *Bahrain: Reform, Security, and U.S. Policy*, Washington, D.C.: Congressional Research Service, January 5, 2011a.

———, *The United Arab Emirates (UAE): Issues for U.S. Policy*, Washington, D.C.: Congressional Research Service, March 10, 2011b.

———, *Oman: Reform, Security, and U.S. Policy*, Washington, D.C.: Congressional Research Service, April 13, 2011c.

———, *Kuwait: Security, Reform, and U.S. Policy*, Washington, D.C.: Congressional Research Service, April 26, 2011d.

Koring, Paul, and Borzou Daragahi, "The Canadian Forces Base at Camp Mirage Is Having Trouble Staying Under Wraps," *The Globe and Mail*, May 21, 2005, reprinted at: http://www.persiangulfonline.org/takeaction/news0605-2.htm

Krepinevich, Andrew, and Robert O. Work, *A New Global Defense Posture for the Second Transoceanic Era*, Washington, D.C.: Center for Strategic and Budgetary Assessments, 2007.

Layne, Christopher, "From Preponderance to Offshore Balancing: America's Future Grand Strategy," *International Security*, Vol. 22, No. 1, Summer 1997, pp. 86–124.

————, "Offshore Balancing Revisited," *Washington Quarterly*, Vol. 24, No. 2, Spring 2002, pp. 233–248.

Mearsheimer, John J., *The Tragedy of Great Power Politics*, New York: W.W. Norton & Company, 2001.

National Center for Ecological Analysis and Synthesis, A Global Map of Human Impacts to Marine Ecosystems: Commercial Activity (Shipping) Data Set, Goleta, Calif.: University of California, Santa Barbara, 2008.

National Defense University, 2011 Worldwide Posture Conference, June 14–15, 2011.

Office of the Secretary of Defense, *Military and Security Developments Involving the People's Republic of China 2011*, Washington, D.C., 2011. As of December 2, 2011: http://www.defense.gov/pubs/pdfs/2011_cmpr_final.pdf

Panetta, Leon E., speech delivered at the Shangri-La Hotel, Singapore, June 2, 2012. As of June 18, 2012: http://www.defense.gov/speeches/speech.aspx?speechid=1681

Parrish, Karen, "Panetta Outlines U.S. Troop Changes in Europe," press release, U.S. Department of Defense, February 16, 2012. As of February 23, 2012: http://www.defense.gov/news/newsarticle.aspx?id=67232

Posen, Barry R., "Command of the Commons: The Military Foundation of U.S. Hegemony," *International Security*, Vol. 28, No. 1, 2003, pp. 5–46.

Posen, Barry R., and Andrew L. Ross, "Competing Visions for U.S. Grand Strategy," *International Security*, Vol. 21, No. 3, Winter 1996/1997, pp. 7–14.

Rollins, John, *Al Qaeda and Affiliates: Historical Perspective, Global Presence, and Implications for U.S. Policy*, Washington, D.C.: Congressional Research Service, CRS-R41070, February 5, 2010. As of December 1, 2011: http://fpc.state.gov/documents/organization/137015.pdf

U.S. Department of Defense, *National Defense Strategy*, Washington, D.C., June 2008.

————, *Quadrennial Defense Review Report*, Washington, D.C., February 2010a.

————, *Nuclear Posture Review Report*, Washington, D.C., April 2010b.

————, *Unclassified Report on the Military Power of Iran*, Washington, D.C., April 2010c.

————, *Base Structure Report Fiscal Year 2011 Baseline*, Washington, D.C., 2011a. As of February 23, 2012: http://www.acq.osd.mil/ie/download/bsr/bsr2011baseline.pdf

————, *2011 U.S. Global Defense Posture Report to Congress*, Washington, D.C., May 2011b.

————, "Sustaining U.S. Global Leadership: Priorities for 21st Century Defense," Washington, D.C., January 2012.

————, "Defense Budget Priorities and Choices," Washington, D.C., January 2012.

Vick, Alan J., and Jacob L. Heim, *Assessing U.S. Air Force Basing Options in East Asia*, Santa Monica, Calif.: RAND Corporation, MG-1204-AF, forthcoming.

Waltz, Kenneth, *Theory of International Politics*, New York: McGraw Hill, 1979.

The White House, *National Security Strategy*, Washington, D.C., May 2010.

Whitlock, Craig, "U.S. Expands Secret Intelligence Operations in Africa," *Washington Post*, June 13, 2012. As of June 18, 2012:
http://www.washingtonpost.com/world/national-security/us-expands-secret-intelligence-operations-in-africa/2012/06/13/gJQAHyvAbV_story.html